Pebble

Weather

Sunshine

Revised Edition

by Gail Saunders-Smith

Content Consultant:
Ken Barlow, Chief Meteorologist
KARE-TV, Minneapolis
Member, American Meteorological Society

CAPSTONE PRESS
a capstone imprint

Pebble Books are published by Capstone Press,
1710 Roe Crest Drive, North Mankato, Minnesota 56003.
www.mycapstone.com

Library of Congress Cataloging-in-Publication Data is available on the Library of
Congress website.

ISBN: 978-1-5157-5968-3 (revised paperback)
ISBN: 978-1-5157-5980-5 (ebook pdf)

Note to Parents and Teachers

The Weather series supports national science standards related to earth
science. This book describes and illustrates how sunshine affects the weather
on earth. The photographs support early readers in understanding the text.
The repetition of words and phrases helps early readers learn new words.
This book also introduces early readers to subject-specific vocabulary
words, which are defined in the Glossary. Early readers may need
assistance to read some words and to use the Table of Contents, Glossary,
Read More, Internet Sites, and Index/Word List sections of the book.

Printed and bound in the United States of America.
009826R

Table of Contents

Sunshine is light from the sun. Sunshine gives the earth light and heat. Sunshine also makes weather on the earth.

Light from the sun travels to the earth in rays. The rays heat the atmosphere. Atmosphere is the air around the earth.

Sunshine falls on one-half of the earth at a time. It is day on one side of the earth. It is night on the other side. The earth spins. It moves places into and out of the light.

The equator is halfway between the top and the bottom of the earth. Sunshine is strongest at places near the equator. At noon, the sun is straight up in the sky. Sunshine makes the air very hot at the equator.

Sunshine is weaker at places near the top and the bottom of the earth. The sun does not go up very high in the sky. Sunshine does not heat the air as much. These places have ice and snow all year long.

Sunshine makes the seasons on the earth. In June, the top of the earth points toward the sun. More sunshine hits the top half of the earth. It is summer here. Less sunshine hits the bottom half of the earth. It is winter there.

In December, the top of the earth points away from the sun. Less sunshine hits the top half of the earth. It is winter here. More sunshine hits the bottom half of the earth. It is summer there.

Sunshine heats the atmosphere. The rays of the sun heat some places more than others. This causes pockets of colder air and pockets of warmer air. These air pockets move and make wind.

Sunshine also heats bodies of water on the earth. The water evaporates. To evaporate means to go into the air. The water in the air gathers into clouds. The clouds carry water around the earth.

Glossary

atmosphere—the air around the earth

equator—places on the earth that are halfway between the top and the bottom of earth are on the equator

evaporate—when something wet goes into the air; when water evaporates, it turns into vapor.

season—one of the four parts of a year; spring, summer, autumn, and winter.

weak—not strong

Read More

Fowler, Allan. *Energy from the Sun*. Rookie Read-About Science. New York: Children's Press, 1997.

Grazzini, Francesca. *Sun, Where Do You Go*? Brooklyn, N.Y.: Kane/Miller Book Publishers, 1996.

Owen, Andy. *Sunshine*. What Is Weather? Des Plaines, Ill.: Heinemann Library, 1999.

Vogt, Gregory L. *The Sun*. Gateway Solar System. Brookfield, Conn.: Millbrook Press, 1996.

Internet Sites

FactHound offers a safe, fun way to find Internet sites related to this book. All of the sites on FactHound have been researched by our staff.

Here's how:

1. Visit *www.facthound.com*

2. Type in this special code **9781560657804** for age-appropriate sites. Or enter a search word related to this book for a more general search.

3. Click on the **Fetch It** button.

FactHound will fetch the best sites for you!

Index/Word List

Word Count: 309
Early-Intervention Level: 23

Editorial Credits
Lois Wallentine, editor; Timothy Halldin, designer; Michelle L. Norstad, photo researcher

Photo Credits
Shutterstock: Anest, 6, BlueOrange Studio, 10, Brian Lasenby, 20, Chermen Otaraev, 18, Golden Pixels LLC, 14, joyfull, 4, JT Platt, 1, Roman Mikhailiuk, cover, smalldaruma, 16, Smolych Iryna, 8, Yegor Larin, 12